THE POCKET LIBRARY OF GREAT ART

Plate 1.   SELF-PORTRAIT. *1878. Oil*
Collection Jakob Goldschmidt, New York

EDOUARD

MANET

(1832–1883)

text by

S. LANE FAISON, Jr.

Chairman, Art Department
Williams College, Williamstown, Mass.

published by HARRY N. ABRAMS, INC., *in association*
with POCKET BOOKS, INC., *New York*

On the cover
detail of A BAR AT THE FOLIES-BERGERE (*plates 28 & 29*)

Plate 2. A BAR AT THE FOLIES-BERGERE. *1881. Oil sketch Boymans Museum, Rotterdam (see plates 28 & 29)*

Ed. Manet,

The sense of detachment is perhaps the dominant expressive element in Manet's art. His is the considered appraisal, the distant contemplation. Influenced by Goya, by Courbet, and by his own contemporaries, the Impressionists, Manet differs radically from all of them. Not for him was Goya's dark sensuality, or Courbet's blunt force, or Renoir's pagan abandon, or Claude Monet's massive effects, or Pissarro's modest intimacy, or Sisley's aerial charm. He was close to the Impressionist circle, yet he did not exhibit with them. Although the most stylish of all the great painters of the nineteenth century, he did not live to see the public recognize him as one of the major recorders of the Parisian life of his time. His very detachment was a barrier to recognition.

Of all the artists whom Manet resembles, Edgar Degas, two years his junior, is the closest in time; and Velasquez, though of the seventeenth century, is the closest in impact. Neither Degas nor Manet can be thought of apart from the city of Paris. Both were aristocrats by temperament, though not by birth. Manet's father, a magistrate, and his mother were altogether bourgeois, as his early portrait of them (plate 3) makes abundantly clear.

The detachment that marks both Degas and Manet found its expression in an extreme aesthetic sensibility. However impressive they may have been as illustrators of the life of their time—and here Degas surpassed Manet—they both insisted on fitting what they saw of the brilliant passing show into a language of pattern, of attenuated shape, of infinitely subtle color relationships disengaged from a particular moment in time. At heart they were both—to use a modern term—abstract artists. While they responded to the elegant aspects of Parisian life, Manet was almost never caustic, as Degas so often became. Unlike Manet, who accepted charm with enthusiasm, Degas explored the beauty of ugliness. For him the rhythm of the ballet and the rhythm of two women ironing were a similar experience, and in neither case were the protagonists physically attractive. Manet, on the contrary, sought out elegance wherever it could be found, not only in the world of fashion and the demimonde, but even in the naked body of a prostitute. "Olympia" (see plates 15 & 16) was his title for her, no doubt to suggest that he wished to idealize her, despite his uncompromis-

Plate 3. PORTRAIT OF THE ARTIST'S PARENTS. *1860. Oil
Collection Mme. E. Rouart, Paris*

Plate 4.   THE OLD MUSICIAN. 1862. *Oil National Gallery of Art,*

ing projection of her shamelessness. Critics who missed the elegance of Olympia's posture, the beauty of texture and pattern, the sophisticated repeat of minor accents, compared her to a stripped fowl.

Among the examples of Degas' influence on Manet, we may cite the connection between his painting, *The Collector of Prints,* dated 1866, and the *Portrait of Emile Zola* which Manet painted two years later (plate 13). It is clear that Manet borrowed Degas' compositional scheme, especially in the arrangement of the background details. The interpretations differ, however; Manet elevates Degas' homely directness to a plane of social distinction, even though Zola himself hardly provided the occasion for such a metamorphosis. Manet's portrait of his friend Antonin Proust, even more than the Zola portrait, strikes Manet's own pose of the *boulevardier*. As we have said in the comment on the Zola portrait, such portraits by Manet were to a considerable degree self-portraiture.

A self-portrait (plate 1) done by Manet in 1878 provides evidence for these conclusions, as do several informal pencil portraits which Degas did of him, three of them now in The Metropolitan Museum of Art. Degas, however, refuses to flatter his friend and eliminates all the glitter. Indeed, he made an etching of Manet which emphasizes a rather fierce expression, something Manet never disclosed in his self-portraits.

Over a period of several years, until he went to Spain in 1865, Manet painted a series of "Spanish" pictures. He attended performances by Spanish dancers in Paris, sought their acquaintance, and made paintings of them, both in groups and individually. *Lola de Valence,* in the Louvre, is the finest. He dressed his brothers, his friends, and his models in Spanish costume, and painted pictures that rival Velasquez in splendor. He imagined bullfights,

Plate 5. THE BATTLE OF THE "KEARSARGE" AND THE "ALABAMA"
1864. Oil. The John G. Johnson Collection, Philadelphia

but with none of Goya's gore. Victorine Meurend, who posed for the *Olympia* and the *Luncheon on the Grass,* masquerades as an *espada* in the arena. In one of his compositions, the figure of a dead toreador stretched out in the foreground had so little connection with the surrounding scene that Manet, yielding for once to the protests of the Salon critics, cut it out as a separate picure. This figure, now in the National Gallery of Art ,Washington, recalls one by Velasquez which he may have seen at a dealer's in Paris. A part of the upper section of the original picture, showing the barrier of the bull ring, is now in The Frick Collection, New York.

It is significant that Manet stopped painting "Spanish" pictures after he went to Spain. A Spain which he knew only through literature and the museums and through itinerant dancers could and did become the means of his early detachment from the life around him. Later, when reality broke the spell of romance, he could join his friends, the Impressionists, in their enthusiasm for themes of contemporary life, and yet at the same time maintain that aesthetic distance from his subject which was so essential to his own expression.

It is also significant that Manet chose to emulate Velasquez, among Spanish painters. Velasquez had been rediscovered by Goya after a century or more of neglect, and it was probably Goya's etchings after Velasquez that first drew Manet's attention to him. Original oil paintings by Velasquez were rare in the Paris of Manet's day, but it is a cardinal rule of art history that artists of the same spiritual family manage to discover one another despite the most difficult obstacles. What attracted Manet to Velasquez was the language of texture and of pattern, of subtle tonalities of gray and black, and the completely impersonal air. What Henri Focillon has said of Manet

Plate 6. **DEAD CHRIST WITH ANGELS.** *1864. Oil*
The Metropolitan Museum of Art, New York

can also be applied to Velasquez: he saw contemporary life "less with abandon and sympathy than with a kind of cruel charm."

The development of Manet's art over a period of about twenty years, from the early *Luncheon on the Grass* (1863, plate 12), to his last important work, the *Bar at the Folies-Bergère* (plates 28 & 29), is studied in some detail in the comments which follow. If space had permitted, we should have said something of Manet as a painter of history, in which he is not outstanding, and as a painter of flowers and of landscape, in which he is. We should also have considered Manet's constant but unfulfilled desire for recognition by the public at large, which partly explains his refusal to exhibit with the circle of Impressionists and his persistence in submitting paintings to the annual Salon despite the most hostile reception. On one occasion he yielded to the pressure of public taste, and in a spirit of rivalry with Frans Hals, painted *Good Bock Beer* (plate 7).

Typical of Manet's turn of mind was the half-facetious Latin pun which he made on his own name: *Manet et manebit* ("He remains and will remain"). He was a good prophet. His work has lasted well, so well that Paul Jamot could write of him, on the occasion of the great retrospective exhibition in Paris which marked the centennial of his birth: "Manet understood instinctively that art, since it is our surest and even our sole means of conquering death, seeks for permanence. Even when the taste and the preoccupations of the day were influencing painters to analyze what is fugitive and to capture what is evanescent, a great artist was able to transform the ephemeral according to the measure of things which are changeless. To the things of this earth where nothing lasts, he brought the sign of eternity."

Plate 7. GOOD BOCK BEER (THE ENGRAVER BELLOT)
1873. Oil. Collection Carroll S. Tyson, Philadelphia

Plate 8.   PORTRAIT OF LINE CAMPINEANU. *1878. Oil*
Nelson-Atkins Gallery, Kansas City (W. R. Nelson Coll.)

COLOR PLATES

PLATE 9

Painted about 1858

BOY WITH CHERRIES

National Gallery of Art, Washington, D. C.
(Gulbenkian Collection, Loan)

25¾ x 21½"

This is one of Manet's earliest works, done when he was about twenty-five, and shortly after he had completed six years of study under Thomas Couture. While it betrays Couture's influence in the carefully graded modeling, notable in the face of the boy, his collar, and the three cherries hanging at the lower left, it is easy to see that Manet is already well launched on his career. The bold scale, the aggressively frontal position of the figure, the insistence on the reds and greens as color areas with intrinsic appeal, and the perfect placement and diagonal balance of the units of design are all characteristic of Manet's style.

The theme of a figure leaning over a wall derives from Dutch art, of which Manet was an ardent student. If the boy were blowing soap bubbles, this work would closely resemble a composition by the eighteenth-century French painter, Chardin, who was likewise attracted to Dutch art. In 1867 Manet actually painted the soap-bubble theme, but the picture (also in the Gulbenkian Collection) is not so close as this one to Chardin's arrangement.

PLATE 10

Painted in 1863

MLLE VICTORINE IN THE COSTUME OF AN ESPADA

The Metropolitan Museum of Art, New York

65½ x 50¾"

This is one of the "Spanish" pictures painted before Manet went to Spain. It is strongly influenced by the romantic enthusiasm for Spain as an exotic land, prevalent in literary circles. Victor Hugo's *Les Orientales* (1829), *Ruy Blas,* and *Hernani* had established this vogue, while Prosper Merimée had popularized it in 1846 with *Carmen,* which Bizet was to set to music in 1875.

As in *The Fifer Boy* (next plate), Manet has posed Victorine, his favorite model, with little regard for anything but a fine composition. The areas of lemon yellow, light blue, lavender, and pink (echoed in a pale variation in the stockings), all set next to the black of the costume, brilliantly project the figure forward, while the remaining elements of the scene retreat in their neutral grays and tans. Victorine's shoes provide the necessary transition in color.

PLATE II

Painted in 1866

THE FIFER BOY

The Louvre, Paris

38½ x 23½"

The jury that rejected this picture from the Salon of 1866 knew what it was doing. Charges of vulgarity which had greeted the *Luncheon on the Grass* (next plate) three years before were not inspired entirely by its combination of fully dressed males and a nude female. A more fundamental opposition, especially on the part of the critics, was aroused by Manet's use of flat tones edged by a thin strip of very dark shadow, instead of the carefully graded procedure taught in art schools for modeling a form from dark to light. Manet's rejection of this process had become particularly clear in *Olympia* (plates 15 & 16), which, though painted in 1863, had first been exhibited at the Salon of 1865, where it was the scandal of the show.

From this more technical point of view, *The Fifer Boy* was an even greater affront to the public's expectation than the *Olympia* had been. Here the whole figure appears to exist on the picture surface like a poster. Black outlines and sharp edges mark off the color areas. There is nothing behind the figure, not even a corner in a bare room. On what do the feet cast their shadows?

Except for the color itself, this is all but a Fauve painting of 1905.

Plate 12.   LUNCHEON ON THE GRASS

(commentary follows color plate section)

PLATE 13

Painted in 1868

PORTRAIT OF EMILE ZOLA

The Louvre, Paris (Bequest of Mme. Zola)

57¼ x 43¼"

Manet painted this portrait out of gratitude for the support Zola had given him in critical reviews. The objects in the picture refer, therefore, to interests which the two men shared. Japanese art, echoed in the screen to the left and the print of an actor to the right, had quickly come into fashion following the 1867 World's Fair in Paris. Velasquez' leadership in steadfast observation of humble people, here represented by a print of *The Topers,* was strikingly prophetic of the naturalistic movement. The print itself is almost certainly the etching which Goya made of Velasquez. Goya was a second force behind the "Spanish" pictures which Manet painted in the early 1860's, before he went to Spain. The name of Manet on the light blue book identifies it as a copy of Zola's essays on him, which had just been republished in a single volume. In them, Zola specifically defended *Olympia,* which appears just above the book in the proxy of a sepia photograph.

Comparison of this portrait with many existing records of Zola's appearance leads to the surprising conclusion that it is more of a self-portrait than a resemblance to Manet's friend and champion.

PLATE 14

Painted in 1869

THE BALCONY

The Louvre, Paris

67¾ x 49¼"

Although this painting was inspired by Goya's *Majas on a Balcony,* nothing could better clarify Manet's procedure than a comparison of the two. Where Goya is murky and sinister, Manet is urbane and elegant. Where Goya strikes a fundamental sexual contrast, Manet contrives a formal pictorial arrangement out of a group of friends taking the air.

The brunette with the penetrating gaze is Berthe Morisot, who later became Manet's sister-in-law. Her natural distinction as a person and her subtlety as a painter both drew Manet's profound admiration. Behind her is the painter Antoine Guillemet, a minor figure in the Impressionist movement. To the right is Jenny Claus, a violinist.

Manet's image of Berthe Morisot has no hint of the sensuality of Goya. Instead, he has conjured up a vision of diaphanous charm *à la* Gainsborough, but unlike Gainsborough has strengthened it with the force of an abstract structure. The balcony, which in Goya's picture fences in the human passions and is properly dark, here establishes the prevailing tonality of green. It also sets up expectations of a formal organization in narrow rectangles and acute triangles, which the reader may discover for himself.

Painted in 1863

OLYMPIA

The Louvre, Paris

51½ x 73¾"

Manet exhibited this painting at the Salon of 1865, two years after he had painted it. The public, already shocked by the combination of nudity and full dress in the *Luncheon on the Grass* (plate 12), considered this display of nakedness altogether scandalous. Here the white flesh of a prostitute is made the more emphatic by contrast to a black string tie, a negro servant, and a sleekly sensual black cat. Critics and public alike felt insulted by the flatness of these shapes, because they were used to carefully rounded forms, modeled according to the precepts of the Academy. Today we can understand the violence of the reaction if we reflect that modern art—in the sense of a denial of photographic illusion and the affirmation of painting as color applied to a flat surface —dates from this and similar works of Manet.

LIFT FOLD FOR ENTIRE PAINTING —
DETAIL AT RIGHT

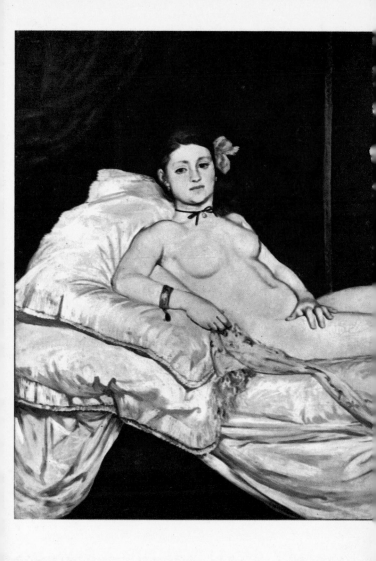

PLATE 17

Painted in 1873

THE RAILWAY

Collection Horace O. Havemeyer, New York

37¼ x 45"

Manet painted this picture from a garden on the rue de Rome, overlooking the Saint-Lazare railroad station. His friend Claude Monet preferred to paint the station itself, with its bustle, its billowing smoke, and the grandiose enclosure of its glass frame. Characteristically, Manet stands at a distance: industry is but a backdrop for a tender and haunting poem. While the woman looks up at us from her book, the child, a prisoner of her dreams, gazes through the iron fence bars.

As he so often contrived to do, Manet has created a strong and abstract design on which to anchor the poetry of his impression. The scale is bold, and the rhythm is not finicky. A wonderfully fresh blue, developed in many variations, pervades the whole canvas. The color selection is as arbitrary as the gridiron pattern of the fence, against which the curves of the woman and child play with such effect. It is probably no accident that the woman's hands, the dog, and the book form an X-shaped design which closely parallels the bow at the girl's back. Such echoes might be called visual metaphors.

PLATE 18

Painted in 1874

BOATING AT ARGENTEUIL

Museum of Fine Arts, Tournai, Belgium

$58\frac{5}{8} \times 44\frac{1}{8}"$

From about 1874, Manet's painting is marked by the broken color and bright palette found in the work of his Impressionist associates. But he by no means abandoned the traditional claims of pictorial design for effects of poetic evanescence.

In this, one of his finest boating scenes, everything is in apparent flux: touches of the brush deposit little glints of light on multiple surfaces. On further observation, however, a formidable structure begins to emerge. The big L of mast and parapet frames a lesser one, defined by the vertical axis of the woman, primly straight, and the line of the man's arm and the folded umbrella he holds. A small but powerful echo of the L motive, inverted, terminates the composition at the lower right. Another L, formed by the boom of the sailboat and placed on the diagonal in depth, is the chief means of connecting foreground and background.

Plate 19. THE EXECUTION OF EMPEROR MAXIMILIAN

(commentary follows color plate section)

PLATE 20

Painted about 1875

BLONDE WITH NUDE BUST

The Louvre, Paris

31⅛ x 23¼"

Superficially, at least, it is hard to believe that this milk-blonde nude was painted by the same artist who gave us the *Olympia* (plates 15 & 16). It is even more disconcerting to discover that Victorine Meurend, Manet's favorite and deeply admired model, posed for the bony asperities of the *Olympia,* while a professional whom he painted only once or twice again served him for this lovely evocation, all wistful and warm. Here the flesh tones, the ocher hair, and the pale blue eyes—their color tied to the blue accents in the fallen chemise—all these blonde harmonies are set against a springtime green to suggest a kind of human flower.

In this later phase of his career, Manet grew increasingly sympathetic to the poetic enchantments evoked by his friends the Impressionists. Gone until his very last years, in paintings like *A Bar at the Folies-Bergère* (plates 28 & 29), were the somber overtones of his early works, of which *Olympia* is a major example.

Painted in 1868

LUNCHEON IN THE STUDIO

Bavarian State Painting Collections, Munich

47¼ x 69"

The rich dark color of the boy's coat projects from the slate grays and white of the background. Its velvet sheen is framed between textures: glass, porcelain, and metal on the left; oysters, china, glass, and the oily surface of a lemon on the right. These are arranged in depth, unlike the books and the pictures on the wall in the Zola portrait (plate 13). An alcove of space is thus formed for the main figure, which is further sharpened by outline and by crisp pockets of cast shadow. Note how the straw hat, the necktie, and the trousers correspond in color and in salience. The faintly marked lapels, however, subtly lace this figure into a series of crossing diagonals into which fit the lemon, the table knife, and the arms of the man and woman.

On the right side of the picture, Manet has elaborated a favorite color contrast: clear, pale blue (china), and leaden olive (oysters).

People sometimes complain that nothing is happening in many Manets. These are the best ones.

LIFT FOLD FOR ENTIRE PAINTING →

DETAIL AT RIGHT

PLATE 23

Painted in 1877

NANA

Museum, Hamburg

60⅝ x 45¼"

It would be tempting to pair this work with Manet's portrait of Zola (plate 13), painted nine years earlier, and so link it to Zola's great novel of the same name. The painting, however, preceded the novel by two years, and actually the Nanas of Zola and Manet could hardly be further apart.

We have already seen that the portrait of Zola has less to do with Zola than with Manet himself. The same distinction between physical force and suave urbanity occurs in the two Nanas. Zola's is a very concrete symbol of lust. Manet's cocotte, although unusually bouncy among his females, is caught in a web of rococo interlace. If she cannot quite match the elegant stance of the heron on the Japanese screen behind her, mocking her so artfully, she is eminently satisfactory for the dressy *boulevardier* at the right. The elegance of this painting lies less in the personality of Nana than in Manet's own touch. The surfaces sparkle and gleam, the blacks are all but transparent. The brush has dragged the paint over the canvas with consummate delicacy.

Plate 24. THE CROQUET MATCH

(commentary follows color plate section)

Plate 25. ON THE BEACH

(commentary follows color plate section)

Painted in 1874

CLAUDE MONET IN HIS "STUDIO"

Bavarian State Painting Collections, Munich

$32\frac{1}{4} \times 39\frac{3}{8}''$

In the summer of 1874, Monet, Renoir, and Manet were all at Argenteuil, on the Seine near Paris. Here they painted several portraits of each other with their families and friends. One of the most interesting is Manet's picture of Claude Monet and his wife in the bark which Monet used as a summer studio. Since light on water is an essential theme of Impressionism, no matter what the actual subject may be, this documentation of Monet's practice is especially precious.

The year 1874 marked the first group show of the circle which from that time came to be known as the Impressionists. We must remember that Manet refused to exhibit with this group, although he was allied to them by many interests and by the ties of intimate friendship. Outdoor themes, unusual in Manet's early work, become much more common from about this date, and the attitude—as in this painting and *Boating at Argenteuil* (plate 18)—is gayer and more carefree.

LIFT FOLD FOR ENTIRE PAINTING →

DETAIL AT RIGHT

Painted in 1881

A BAR AT THE FOLIES-BERGERE

Courtauld Institute of Art, London

$37\frac{3}{4} \times 50''$

It is instructive to compare this serene masterpiece of Manet's last years with the small oil sketch now in Rotterdam (plate 2). Manet intended to set down as spontaneously as he could a momentary impression, including its image in a mirror. With quick strokes of a heavily loaded brush he accented the animation of the passing show. Except for the rather subdued color, here is the very essence of the Impressionist point of view.

When Manet came to consider the final composition, he regarded Impressionism as no more than a means to an end: to express himself in formally disciplined and traditionally durable terms, as in his work of the 'sixties. Observe what liberties he has taken with appearance, how he has rearranged what he *saw* in order to clarify what he *felt*.

Is the reflected girl the same person who occupies the center of the picture? If so, Manet has shifted his own position as spectator, and thereby destroyed forever the illusion of a single moment in time. This is perhaps the major difference between the impact of the sketch and the final work.

LIFT FOLD FOR ENTIRE PAINTING ⟶

DETAIL AT RIGHT

PLATE 30

Painted in 1878

AT THE CAFE

Walters Art Gallery, Baltimore

18⅝ x 15⅜"

Among all the later works of Manet, this small picture
is the finest of those which can be called, in the strictest
sense of the term, Impressionist. Here even Renoir is
matched, if not surpassed, in vivaciousness, in luminos-
ity, in civilized hedonism. The glasses of beer are concen-
trates of Impressionist sensibility to light refracted in
glass and in liquid. Their flashing tan tonalities, echoed
frequently in this painting, set the major tonal contrast
for the all-important blues.

Part of the verve of this picture is due to its placement
slightly on the diagonal into depth, in contrast to the
strong insistence on frontality of the relatively solemn
Bar at the Folies-Bergère (preceding plates). Note how
the hand of the man (a nineteenth-century detail out of
Van Dyck) balances the beer glass at the left, yet is set
somewhat further back in space in accordance with the
diagonal line of the table. These two motives are further
connected by a continuous curve, which starts at the
handle of the glass of beer, swings down and forward,
then right and across to the far side of the man's hand.
The same curve forms the upper part of the girl who
stands behind the main figures.

PLATE 31

Painted about 1882

PORTRAIT OF IRMA BRUNNER

The Louvre, Paris

Pastel on canvas, 21¼ x 17¾

In the background of *A Bar at the Folies-Bergère* (plates 28 & 29), a woman leaning on the balcony railing has turned her head so that the profile is silhouetted against a circular black hat. The portrait of Irma Brunner is, so to speak, a development of this small detail. Both resemble a finely designed coin.

The *Bar* was Manet's last major work, and this portrait was one of the last of his lesser works. Into it he breathed every subtlety he knew of texture, veiled nuance, and dashing rhythm. The chalk dust of pastel becomes all but moist at the bright lips, where the pale reds of the dress, the flesh tones, and the background are suddenly and vibrantly concentrated. The black hat, lustrous as oil, is a dark foil for a pale jewel. Like certain hats in portraits by Frans Hals, it catches up the circular rhythms of a face, and it deftly describes, in larger scale, a containing arc.

If it were possible to compound Fragonard's freshness with the nobility of profile of an ancient Greek coin, Manet has surely contrived to do it here.

PLATE 32

Painted in 1883

WHITE LILACS AND ROSES

Private Collection, New York

22 x 18"

Just to right of center in *A Bar at the Folies-Bergère* (plates 28 & 29), a glass vase containing two roses stands on a gray marble counter before the rich, dark blue of the girl's dress. *White Lilacs and Roses,* which Manet painted about two years later, is an enlarged development of this detail, just as the *Portrait of Irma Brunner* (preceding plate) derives from the detail of one of the spectators at the upper left of the same composition. Many of Manet's larger works contain still-life arrangements, often in the lower left-hand corner, as in *Boy with Cherries, Luncheon on the Grass,* and *Luncheon in the Studio* (plates 9, 12, 21 & 22).

The potential rigidity of the cross-shaped arrangement is broken up by an inner diagonal cross, with the three fat roses set athwart a long diagonal of greens. The real vitality of the picture, however, comes from the brushwork. Here, on a small scale, is one of Manet's most brilliant late works, but like the *Bar,* it recalls the dark opulence of *Olympia* (plates 15 & 16) and the *Portrait of Zola* (plate 13).

LUNCHEON ON THE GRASS

Painted in 1863. 84½ x 106¼"
The Louvre, Paris

The attempt to translate the French title of this picture,
Déjeuner sur l'herbe, into "Luncheon on the Grass" or
"Picnic in the Woods," merely points up its inappropri-
ateness. Manet called it *Le Bain* (The Bathing Party),
but the public conferred the title which has become in-
separable from this work. Both titles are almost useless:
all bathing is suspended, and no one is concerned about
luncheon. The protagonists are caught in a sort of Egyp-
tian fixity. In the foreground, a magnificent blue still life
provides the key to the whole composition. In effect,
figures and landscape comprise a formal composition
more akin to the aims of still-life painting than the subject itself might suggest.

THE EXECUTION OF
EMPEROR MAXIMILIAN

Painted in 1867. 96½ x 118⅛"
Museum, Mannheim, Germany

That Manet painted this subject at all is something of
a curiosity. He made few excursions into historical or
political themes, and it is clear that they did not move
him. Possibly the account of the execution of the Emperor Maximilian in Mexico, an event of considerable
political import in Paris, turned Manet's thoughts to
Goya. During his trip to Spain two years earlier, Manet
had seen Goya's *Third of May,* which represents the execution of *Madrileños* by Napoleonic troops in 1808.

THE CROQUET MATCH

Painted in 1873. 23⅜ x 41¾"
Staedelsches Kunstinstitut, Frankfurt-am-Main

The development of Manet's art can be profitably studied by comparing this picture with the *Luncheon on the Grass* (plate 12), painted ten years earlier. Under the growing influence of Manet's association with the Impressionists, *The Croquet Match* extends the pull back into space, decreases the scale of the figures, breaks up the areas of color, and infiltrates the whole picture with movement and light. Another change appears in the use of green: rich and strong like Courbet's in the *Luncheon,* tender and muted according to Manet's own delicate sensibility in this later work.

ON THE BEACH

Painted in 1873. 20½ x 28⅜"
Formerly Collection Jacques Doucet, Paris

Painted in the summer of 1873 at Berck, on the Channel below Boulogne-sur-Mer, *On the Beach* is one of Manet's early masterpieces of outdoor Impressionism. Degas and Claude Monet had already designed somewhat similar compositions, but they isolated the figures more sharply in the front plane, with the background a mere suggestion of locale. In Manet, however, the motion, the color, and even the distance of the ocean are alluded to in the foreground. The woman (Mme. Manet) leads us inward to the man (Manet's brother, Eugene), whose thoughts send us scudding across the sand and out to sea.

Plate 33. ADVERTISEMENT FOR CHAMPFLEURY'S "CATS"
About 1869. Lithograph

Plate 34. ILLUSTRATION FOR POE'S "THE RAVEN." *Engraving, 1889, after a wash drawing of 1875. The New York Public Library*

Plate 35. LOLA DE VALENCE. *1862. Etching*
The New York Public Library

Plate 36. THE BARRICADE. *1871. Lithograph*
The New York Public Library

Plate 37.   PORTRAIT OF EVA GONZALES. *1870. Oil*
National Gallery, London

Plate 38. PORTRAIT OF MME. MICHEL LEVY. *1882. Pastel and oil*
National Gallery of Art, Washington, D.C.
(Chester Dale Collection, Loan)

Plate 39. THE DEPARTURE OF THE FOLKESTONE BOAT. 1869. O*il*

Collection Carroll S. Tyson, Philadelphia

Plate 40.   THE RACES AT LONGCHAMP. *1864. Oil*

The Art Institute of Chicago

Plate 41. WOMAN FIXING HER GARTER. *About 1878–80. Pastel*
Hansen Collection, Ordrupgårdsamlingen, Copenhagen

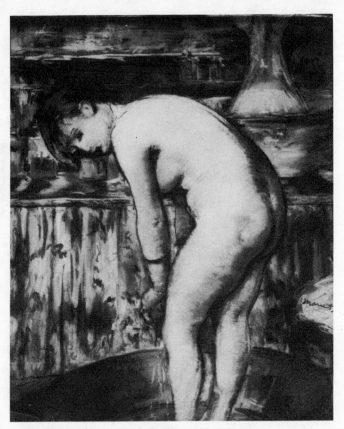

Plate 42.   THE TUB. *About 1878–80. Pastel*
Collection Bernheim jeune, Paris

BIOGRAPHICAL NOTES

1832   Edouard Manet (pronounced *ma-NAY*) born January 23 at Paris. Father, Auguste Manet, was an official in the Ministry of Justice.

1850–56   Studies with Thomas Couture, who is bitterly critical of his student's work. Copies old masters in the Louvre; travels in Italy, the Netherlands, and Germany.

1859   *The Absinthe Drinker,* his first painting submitted to the Salon, is refused.

1863   *Luncheon on the Grass* sets off a scandal at the *Salon des Refusés,* organized by Napoleon III. Marries Suzanne Leenhoff, of Dutch origin.

1865   Trip to Spain.

1871   The dealer Durand-Ruel buys 22 pictures for 35,000 francs (about $8,750 at the time).

1873   *Good Bock Beer* his first success at the Salon.

1874   Spends summer at Argenteuil (near Paris) with Claude Monet and Renoir.

1882   After many years of refusals, he is finally awarded the Cross of the Legion of Honor.

1883   Dies April 30 at Paris. Among the honorary pallbearers are Claude Monet, Emile Zola, and his constant and devoted friend Antonin Proust, now Minister of Fine Arts.

SOME OPINIONS OF THE TIME

Dante Gabriel Rossetti, *Letter,* 1864: "There is a man named Manet to whose studio I was taken by Fantin, whose pictures are for the most part mere scrawls, and who seems to be one of the lights of the school."

Charles Baudelaire, *Letter,* 1865: "Turning on either a small or large amount of heat . . . ridicule, insult, injustice are excellent things, and Manet would be ungrateful if he were not to thank injustice."

Emile Zola, *Mes Haines,* 1867: "Lying deep in his nature, there is an innate need for distinction and elegance which I pride myself on having found again in his works."

Auguste Renoir, *Letter to Manet,* 1881: "I was expecting . . . to see your nomination as Chevalier of the Legion of Honor, which would have brought applause to me on my distant island. . . . You are the happy fighter, without hatred for anyone, like an ancient Gaul; and I like you for that gaiety maintained even in the midst of injustice."

Gustave Geffroy, *La Justice,* Paris, May 3, 1883: "What we can affirm today . . . is the great consequence of the revolution he has made, the influence he has exerted and which he will exert until the day when another original artist will arrive to tell anew to angry crowds who will pelt him with stones in the name of Manet, whose *Olympia* and *Luncheon on the Grass* will then be in the Louvre."

SOME OTHER BOOKS
ABOUT MANET

M. Guérin. *L'oeuvre gravé de Manet*. Paris, Floury, 1944
(Complete account of the graphic work)

Paul Jamot and Georges Wildenstein. *Manet*. Paris, Van
Oest, 1932. Two volumes (Large, detailed catalog
with an important critical introduction)

E. Moreau-Nélaton. *Manet raconté par lui-même*. Paris,
H. Laurens, 1926. Two volumes (The basic biog-
raphy)

John Rewald. *The History of Impressionism*. New York,
The Museum of Modern Art, 1946

Robert Rey. *Manet*. Paris, Hyperion, 1938 (A good short
account with excellent plates)

ACKNOWLEDGMENTS

*In a book of art, it seems particularly fitting to ac-
knowledge the work of craftsmen who contribute to its
making. The color plates were made by Litho-Art,
Inc., New York. The lithography is from the presses
of The Meehan-Tooker Co., Inc., New York and the
binding has been done by F. M. Charlton Co., New
York. The paper was made by P. H. Glatfelter Co.,
Spring Grove, Pa. Our deepest indebtedness is to the
museums, galleries, and private collectors who gra-
ciously permitted the reproduction of their paintings,
drawings, and sculpture.*

*Plates 7, 39, 41, and 42—photographs courtesy of
Wildenstein and Co., New York.*